WHEN GOD SERENADES YOU WITH THE RAIN

GAIL HAWKINS

Inspired by God

JOURNAL JOY

An Imprint of Journal Joy Publishers

www.thejournaljoy.com

Paperback ISBN: 978-1-957751-43-6

Ebook ISBN: 978-1-957751-44-3

Edited by: Nicole Evans

First paperback edition, 2023

DEDICATION:

In loving memory of my mother, Mattie Lois Nickens, who gave me the love and appreciation of the rain. In addition, she continues to inspire me from the clouds above the rain. To my firstborn granddaughter, Harmony Hawkins, who inspires me with her love and energy. May you always see the rain as a refreshing blessing even if it comes during life's storms.

For Trey, Gabrielle, and Hezekiah

When God serenades you with the rain, are you a captive audience member listening?

Do you wake up from your deep sleep and unfinished dreams listening?

Are you excited about the water remnants after its cleansing power leaves things glistening?

When God serenades you with the rain,

do you even notice all the trouble He's going through

just to make things better for you?

When God serenades you with His orchestra of raindrops,

clouds, thunder, and lightning bolts,

is it frightening with each jolt?

Do you appreciate the sounds of the rain?

Each...Drip,

drop,

splish,

splash!

Drip,

drop,

splish,

splash!

Do you hear the beat and want to move your feet? Do you feel

the rhythm of the instruments?

Pitter patter on the windowsill soft and mellow,

until the crescendo erupts with a clap and a clang,

a boom then a bang!

Do you notice the difference the rain makes on the ground and the rooftop, or do you just want it to stop?

Are you annoyed by the pouring rain and the way it drains down the side of the building, or can you enjoy the new puddle that becomes a drum pad for the refrain

When God serenades you with the rain, don't complain and become disdained over things that will be canceled or changed.

Like any orchestra, the preparations aren't in vain when the audience listens to the sound of each note, returning their appreciation with a standing ovation.

When the concert is over, be thankful for what was, as you

anticipate a fresh clean day, so again you can play.

Applaud the Conductor for guiding the instruments of His choice,

directing them without you hearing Him use His voice.

When God serenades you with the rain, praise His marvelous and magnificent name.

God Reigns

AUTHOR PAGE:

Gail Hawkins is a first-time book author who loves nature and writing poetry. Although this is her first published book, she has been writing poetry since the first grade, and loves to read and recite poetry aloud. Her mother's appreciation for the raindrops and snowflakes is the inspiration for this book and many more poems.

Gail Hawkins - A lover of poetry and spoken word. A lover of nature and the beauty of water. *When God Serenades You with the Rain* was inspired by my late mother, Mattie Nickens, and her love for the rain. We would sit on the porch during rain showers and watch thunderstorms from the window. My admiration for God and the beauty of His works also inspired this poem. Being outside in the rain feels like our Creator is touching me as He washes, cleanses, and refreshes the earth. This book celebrates the rain and how we can allow our senses to experience rain from a positive perspective. I hope more rain lovers will be inspired after reading my book.

I hope to write more books about the Weather Maker and read and recite my poetry publicly. As an award-winning Toastmaster, I plan to compete more as a public speaker.

I have been showered with the blessings of being a wife, mother, and grandmother.

Author email: GailHawkins2006@yahoo.com